Titles by Marsha Ward

Fiction:

The Owen Family Saga
Gone for a Soldier
The Man from Shenandoah
Spinster's Folly
Ride to Raton
Trail of Storms

Promised Valley
The Zion Trail

Other Fiction
Blood at Haught Springs
Faith and the Foreman

Nonfiction:

Rapid Recipes for Writers... and Other Busy People

Simple Book List and Purchase Links

marshaward.com/bookshelf/simple-list/

From Julia's Kitchen

Owen Family Cookery

Marsha Ward

WestWard Books
❧ ♦ ☙
Payson, Arizona

From Julia's Kitchen
Owen Family Cookery

Copyright © 2017 Marsha Ward

Cover Design by Linda Boulanger
Tell~Tale Book Covers

ISBN: 9780996146333
ebook ISBN: 9780996146326

WestWard Books
P O Box 53
Payson, Arizona

Table of Contents

INTRODUCTION

I created a fictional family some years ago, the Owen family of Shenandoah County, Virginia, led by father Rod and mother Julia. I've taken them through the hardships and horrors of the American Civil War, and followed their trek west to Colorado Territory thereafter. Daughter Marie took me on an interesting sidetrack, trying to get herself settled and married in her anxiety about getting "too old." Son James left the safety of the homestead in anger, and encountered rough adventures and trials as he struck out alone to find his own way in the world.

A few months ago, I had a wild idea: why not prepare a collection of recipes, or as they were often known, receipts, from an earlier America, that reflected meals and dishes Julia Owen might have cooked for her family? Finding suitable ones has been an adventure, and quite a dive into earlier times and methods of cookery, both before and after the iron kitchen range—that is, a combined stove and oven made of iron—was readily available.

Julia ran through quite a lot of different cookery means for preparing meals. She cooked on an iron range for her brother at their home in Pennsylvania. Then, married and settled in Virginia, she cooked for a time in a fireplace with an oven built into the wall beside it for baking, and later had a stove in a proper kitchen. Her cookery went back to primitive as she crossed the plains, using a campfire. Once she arrived in Colorado Territory, she again resorted to fireplace cookery.

As her family grew, circumstances and events added to her "receipt" collection. Some she got from friends and some were brought to her after events involving family members. Others came through new situations and acquaintances. I've noted the fictional origins of most of them, that is, how Julia came to have the recipe in her collection.

If you haven't read the novels in The Owen Family Saga, please be aware that there are spoilers in a few of these notes.

Some of the receipts are curiosities, and I've made little or no attempt to alter them for modern cooks. For others, I've made slight changes to accommodate us. However, you won't find crock pot or microwave recipes herein.

I hope you will give several of the recipes a try. May they enlarge your cookery repertoire and enrich your family meals.

A Note on Temperatures

A lot of Julia's cookery was done by the "by guess and by gosh" method, including how hot the oven was. She never had the luxury of an automatic thermostat to regulate the temperature setting for that oven.

Much of the heat regulation was done with the type of wood used. Hard wood was preferred, as it burned hot for a sustained period. Her method of control was to add additional chunks of wood as needed during the cooking, baking or roasting process.

Some recipes baked best in a hot—or "quick"—oven. Others needed a moderate oven, while others only required a low—or "slow"—oven temperature.

The best way Julia had of gauging the current oven temperature was to put her hand inside for a time. When it was no longer tolerable to keep it there, she knew the intensity of heat in her oven and could adjust according to the needs of her recipe:

Low/Slow oven (200°-300° F.) - 60 seconds
Moderate oven (350° F.) - 45 seconds
Hot/Quick oven (400°-450° F.) - 35 seconds

MARSHA WARD

~NOTES~

BEEF & OTHER MEAT AND GAME

Hash

After Julia turned ten years old and was deemed capable enough to keep house, she found this old "receipt" written out by her father's former housekeeper. It was the beginning of her recipe collection.

~~~

One and one-half teacup of boiling water must be poured into a saucepan. Mix one heaping spoonful flour with one tablespoonful cold water, stir it in and boil three minutes. Then add two teaspoonfuls salt, half a small teaspoonful pepper, and butter the size of an egg.

After removing all tough, gristly pieces from the cold cooked meat, chop it fine with some boiled potatoes. Put them in the dressing, heat through, then serve.

Should you have any cold gravy left, use it; in that case you will require less butter, salt and pepper. You can serve it with buttered toast underneath, or you may set it into the oven to brown on top, or drop eggs into a skillet of boiling salt water, and when cooked, place on top of hash.

Baked Ham

When Julia married Rod, she learned many cookery skills from her neighbors. Sometimes she bartered eggs and butter for goods at the Hilbrands' store in Mount Jackson. Here's how she would deal with a cured ham.

~~~

Remove a cured ham from a hogshead and clean off the ashes. Soak the ham in cold water for 2 days and 2 nights, changing the water in that time four times. Wash it thoroughly in tepid water.

Place it skin down in the ham boiler, which must be full of cold water. Do not boil too fast, and as the water boils down, replenish with hot water. When the ham is done it will turn of its own accord skin up in the boiler.

While the ham is hot, remove the skin carefully, then place the ham in a large pan. Stick the ham full of cloves, sprinkle with black pepper, bread crumbs, and brown sugar. Pour over it a cup of sherry wine and put it in the oven until it is nicely baked and browned.

Roast for Sunday Dinner

Julia's seven growing sons appreciated the beef roast she occasionally prepared for Sunday dinners. This is a smaller version for modern cooks.

~ ~ ~

1 7-bone shoulder roast
10 potatoes, quartered
2 onions, cut in eighths
6 carrots, cut up
1 teaspoon salt
1/2 teaspoon pepper
1/2 teaspoon garlic powder
bay leaves
1/2 cup water

Put roast in large oven-proof pan. Add potatoes, onions, carrots, and bay leaves.

Sprinkle spices over the top of everything, then sprinkle with the water to distribute them evenly.

Cover with foil, shiny side down.

Bake in 325° F. oven for 3 1/2 to 4 hours. Serve with vegetables and salad.

Tender, Juicy Beef

Julia acquired this recipe after Rod went to Texas to buy cattle in *The Man from Shenandoah*. The foreman that Rod hired, Bill Henry, showed her how to make a tough cut of beef tender.

~ ~ ~

More than an hour before the sun goes down, build a hot fire in a three-foot-deep hole and let it burn down to coals for one hour.

In the meantime, get an iron pot with a cover that has a projecting rim that prevents ashes from getting into it. Alternate layers of a large tough cut of beef, salt pork, and hard bread. Cover with water.

Shovel the coals from the hole. Place the covered pot in the bottom of the hole. Immediately bury the pot with the coals and cover with a layer of dry earth. Leave to bake all night.

SOUPS & STEWS

Stewed Rabbit

Julia prepared this dish for her father and her brother Jonathan once she was old enough to keep house and do the cooking and baking.

~~~

Cut up the rabbit and wash it. Put it in a stew-pan and season it with salt and pepper. Pour in half a pint of water, and when this has nearly stewed away, add half a pint of chicken stock, one tablespoon of vinegar, one half teaspoon of mace, and a tablespoonful of flour mixed with a quarter pound of butter.

Let it stew gently till quite tender, and then serve hot.

Vegetable Soup

When Aunt Susannah brought her family from Virginia to visit the Helm family in Pennsylvania, Julia learned to prepare this vegetable soup to feed the larger group. I've left the recipe in the original form.

~~~

To make a dinner pot of vegetable soup for a family of seven or eight, put on in cold water 2 pounds beef and boil till tender.

Then add the following, finely cut up: 5 good-sized potatoes, 4 carrots, 1/2 dozen medium-sized turnips, half of a small head of cabbage, 1 can of tomatoes, or the like quantity of fresh ones.

Let all these boil and put more water in when needed.

1 hour before dinner, cut up 2 onions and a bunch of green celery tops and put them in with the other vegetables (if celery is boiled too long it loses its flavor).

Before taking up for dinner, the beef should be cut up in small pieces and returned to the pot.

Chicken Soup & Dumplings

Julia got this receipt from a Pennsylvania neighbor who had been visiting in Maryland, where she acquired it. Start with a plucked and gutted chicken.

~ ~ ~

Put the chicken on in cold water and let it boil till tender. Take it out about an hour before dinner and cut it in pieces and return it to the pot.

Add about 1 pint of milk, a large piece of butter, red pepper, and salt to taste. Also put in a teaspoonful of flour made to a thickening.

Make small balls out of fine pastry and drop them into the soup 20 minutes before serving. Do not remove the lid from the pot until ready to serve, as doing so would make them heavy; and do not let them stand, but serve at once.

Beef Stew

Julia began making this stew in Virginia whenever she had a cut of beef to cook. The recipe has been modernized for our convenience.

~~~

2-4 pounds stew meat or hamburger
12 potatoes, diced
1 large onion, diced
3 stalks celery with tops, chopped
3 or 4 carrots, sliced in wheels or cubes
1 can tomatoes
1 clove garlic, minced
salt
pepper
parsley flakes

Brown the beef in the bottom of a Dutch oven or stock pot. Fill the pot 1/2 full of water.

Cut up the potatoes, carrots, onions, and celery and add to the pot. Add any leftover vegetables or canned vegetables you have around.

Add the canned tomatoes, along with the garlic and seasonings to taste. If the water is low, add enough to fill the pot.

Boil until the potatoes and carrots are done. To thicken the stew, add 2 tablespoons cornstarch to a little cold water; mix; then add to the boiling stew. Repeat as needed.

Or top with dumplings. See recipe for *Baking Powder Biscuits* on page 33.

~NOTES~

Tomato Soup

Rod really relished this soup, which newlywed Julia learned to cook from a young neighbor woman who befriended her, Muriel Bates. He never dared tell Julia he once courted Muriel. Fortunately, he lost out to his best friend, Chester Bates.

~~~

1 quart tomatoes
1 quart water
1 teaspoon soda
1 pint milk
salt
pepper
butter the size of a hen's egg

Put the water and tomatoes on and let boil, then strain through a sieve.

Add the soda, milk, salt, pepper, and butter. Let all boil together.

If you prefer it thinner than this makes it, add water to suit taste.

Brunswick Stew

Sometimes it was necessary to live off the land—or the trees. For this stew, Julia would remove the innards and pluck the chicken or skin the squirrels before cutting them up for the pot. I've left this "receipt" in its original state

~~~

Take one chicken or two squirrels, cut them up and put one half gallon water to them. Let it stew until the bones can be removed.

Add one-half dozen large tomatoes, one-half pint butter-beans, and corn cut from half a dozen ears, salt, pepper, and butter as seasoning.

MARSHA WARD

Brown Soup

Rod brought this throw-together soup
"receipt" home with him after the American
Civil War. Living more or less off the land in
the dark days of the war, the cavalrymen
under his command often didn't have the
right spices at hand, so they improvised
with whatever they could get.

~~~

A knuckle of veal
3 quarts water
thyme
parsley
mace
allspice
salt
pepper
browned flour
1 egg yolk
1 tablespoon butter

Simmer veal in water for about four
hours before seasoning, then add the spices,
salt, and pepper. Let simmer two hours
more.

Thicken with browned flour.

Beat the egg yolk and butter together
and stir in after removing soup from the fire.

POULTRY

Boiled Turkey

Julia's father insisted that the turkey hens should be boiled in spring, and the gobblers (male or tom turkeys) roasted in winter.

~ ~ ~

Take a hen turkey, preparing it in the usual way, and fill it with the following dressing: Two eggs beaten with chopped beef suet*, flour enough to make a thick pudding, seasoned with black pepper, salt, and a little butter. Fill the turkey with this, sew up well, and put it in a pot of water and boil until tender.

Mash some flour in drawn (clarified) butter and cold water. Boil it in a vessel to make a thick gravy.

Remove the turkey from the pot to a serving platter. Pour a third of the gravy over the turkey, after which cut up 3 or 4 hard-boiled eggs. Put the eggs over the turkey on top of the thick gravy, then thin the remainder of the gravy with water from the pot in which the turkey was boiled, and serve it with the turkey.

Garnish the dish containing the turkey with carrots cut in rings.

*See the definition of suet in the final chapter on page 61.

17

Roasting Poultry

Julia learned the diverse ways of roasting barnyard fowl early in life.

~~~

Turkey:

Wash the outside and inside very clean.

Take bread crumbs, grated or chopped, about enough to fill the turkey. Chop a bit of salt pork, the size of a good egg, and mix it in, with butter the size of an egg, pepper, salt, and sweet herbs to your taste. Beat up an egg and work in.

Fill the crop and the body, sew them up, and tie the legs and wings. Put the turkey on a spit. Set it where it will gradually heat, and turn it once or twice, while heating, for fifteen minutes. Then put it up to the fire and allow about twenty-five minutes for each pound.

Turkey must be cooked very thoroughly. It must roast slowly at first, and be often basted with butter on a fork. Dredge with flour just before taking it up, and let it brown.

Put the inwards [giblets] in a skillet to boil for two hours, chop them up, season them, use the liquor [liquid] they are boiled in for gravy, and thicken it with brown flour and a bit of butter, the size of a hen's egg. This is the giblet sauce.

Take the drippings, say half a pint,

thickened with a paste made of a tablespoonful of brown or white flour, and let it simmer five minutes, and then use it for thin gravy.

Roast Goose

A goose should be roasted in the same manner as a turkey. It is better to make the stuffing of mashed potatoes, seasoned with salt, pepper, sage, and onions, to the taste. Apple sauce is good to serve with it. Allow fifteen minutes to a pound for a gosling, and twenty or more for an older one. Goose should be cooked rare.*

Roast Chickens

Wash them clean outside and inside, stuff them as directed for turkeys, baste them with butter, lard, or drippings, and roast them about an hour.

Chickens should be cooked thoroughly.

Stew the inwards [giblets] till tender, and till there is but little water. Chop them and mix in gravy from the dripping-pan, thicken with brown flour, and season with salt, pepper, and butter. Cranberry, or new-made applesauce, is good with them.

Modern science might disagree.

Roast Ducks

Wash the ducks, and stuff them with a dressing made with mashed potatoes wet with milk, and chopped onions, sage, pepper, salt, and a little butter, to suit your taste.

Reserve the inwards [giblets] to make the gravy, as is directed for turkeys, except it should be seasoned with sage and chopped onions.

Ducks will cook in about an hour, as they are to be cooked rare.* Baste them with salt water, and before taking up, dredge on a little flour and let it brown.

Green peas and stewed cranberries are good accompaniments.

Canvass-back ducks are cooked without stuffing. Wild ducks must be soaked in salt and water the night previous, to remove the fishy taste, and then in the morning put in fresh water, which should be changed once or twice.

* *Modern science might disagree.*

Pigeon

Julia learned to cook pigeons after she married and lived in Virginia.

~~~

Pigeons are good stuffed and roasted, or baked. They are better stewed thus:

Stuff them like turkeys. Put them in a pot, breast downwards. Cover them with salted water an inch above the top, and simmer, two hours if tender, and three if tough.

When nearly done, stir in a bit of butter the size of a goose egg, for every dozen pigeons. Take them up and add a little flour paste to the gravy [residue in the pot], with salt and pepper. Pour some of the gravy over the pigeons, and put the rest in a gravy dish.

Creamed Chicken

A "company" recipe Julia got from Mrs. Hilbrands.

~~~

1 pound cold chicken or turkey
2 ounces butter
2 tablespoons flour
1 pint milk
salt
red and black pepper
1 glass Sherry wine
2 hard-boiled eggs, chopped fine

Cut the chicken as for salad. Rub butter into the flour.

Cover the chicken with the milk and let it get hot. Stir in the butter and flour, salt, peppers, and wine. When ready to serve, stir in the eggs and serve at once, very hot.

Chicken Pie

Julia raised chickens in Virginia and in Colorado, both for egg production and for meat.

~~~

Joint and boil two chickens in salted water, just enough to cover them, and simmer slowly for half an hour.

Line a dish with pie crust.

Dredge the chicken in a little flour. Layer the chicken (seasoning each layer with salt and pepper), with thin slices of broiled pork and butter the size of a goose egg cut in small pieces. Put in enough of the liquid in which the meat was boiled, to reach the surface (cover the chicken).

Cover all with a light, thick crust. Make a small slit in the center of the crust. Bake about one hour in a hot oven (400-450° F.). If it begins to scorch, lay a paper over it a short time.

~NOTES~

DRIED BEANS

Boiled Beans

Julia fed her growing family on plenty of beans and cornbread.

~ ~ ~

Soak beans overnight. Next morning, soak in fresh water till two hours before dinner, then drain and put them into a saucepan of boiling water, and cook them, covered, for two hours.

Drain and add a large spoonful of fresh butter, and a little salt.

A little saleratus* added to the soaking water improves old beans; a piece as big as a pea will do. If you put in too much, the skins will slip off.

See the definition of saleratus in the final chapter on page 61.

Baked Beans

When Rulon went to earn money to pay the minister for performing his marriage ceremony in *Gone for a Soldier*, he brought back this recipe, which he gave to Julia, who in turn passed it along to her daughter-in-law, Mary. Serves six, or four hungry men.

~~~

Bake beans in an iron pot with a cover that has a projecting rim. This prevents ashes from getting into the pot.

Parboil a quart and a half of dry beans in a large pot in one or two waters until the outside skin starts to crack.

Put the beans into the baking pot. Gash the rind of a pound of salt pork so it will cut easily after baking. Place the pork just under the surface of the beans. Add two or three tablespoonsful of molasses and a little salt, unless the pork is considerably lean. Add enough water to cover the beans.

Dig a hole in the ground three or more feet deep, and heat for an hour by a good hot fire. Shovel out the coals and put the pot in the bottom. Immediately bury it with the coals, and cover all with dry earth. Leave the beans to bake all night.

Beans with Cheese

Tom O'Connor, the blacksmith who came west with the Owen family in *The Man from Shenandoah*, married a young lady of Hispanic descent after he settled in Leones, as we learned in *Ride to Raton*. This recipe was a favorite of Rosalinda's family, and got shared around the community of Shenandoah neighbors.

~~~

2 cups pinto beans
6 cups water
1/2 cup lard or shortening
1/2 cup shredded cheddar or jack cheese
salt

Combine beans and water in a large saucepan. Simmer. Cover pot and cook slowly until tender, about 2 1/2 to 3 hours. Stir often, salting to taste during last half hour of cooking.

Pots vary; so if the liquid gets low, add boiling water.

When done, don't drain the pot. Remove the excess liquid with a ladle and set it aside.

Add the lard, stirring until melted. Leave the cover off and simmer for 30 minutes, stirring frequently.

If the beans get dry, add enough of the reserved liquid to make a thick soup. Add cheese, heating until it melts, and serve.

~NOTES~

MEXICAN DISHES

Pedernales River Chili

Rod brought this recipe home from his abortive adventure in the U.S. War with Mexico. The recipe yields 2 1/2 quarts.

~~~

4 pounds coarsely ground chuck
1 large onion, chopped
2 cloves garlic, crushed
2 tablespoons chili powder
2 teaspoons salt
1 teaspoon cumin, seed or powder
1 teaspoon oregano
2 1-pound cans tomatoes
2 cups hot water

In large skillet, cook together meat, onion, and garlic until meat changes color. Add chili powder, salt, oregano, cumin, tomatoes and hot water; mix well. Simmer about 1 hour, skimming fat.

Corn Tortillas

These are the same corn tortillas Amparo made for James in *Ride to Raton*, and that Jessie and Luke Bingham ate in *Trail of Storms*, but Marie got the recipe from the cook at the Dominquez brothers' rancho on her way home after the events in *Spinster's Folly*.

~~~

2 cups dry masa harina (finely ground corn flour)
1 1/4 cups water

Combine dry masa harina and water; knead to blend well. If necessary, add a little more water to make dough hold together.

Shape to form 12 balls. Roll out or press each ball between 2 sheets of waxed paper or pat out by hand to form a 6-inch circle.

Bake on a hot, lightly greased griddle until lightly browned on both sides. Serve with beans, using as a spoon, if necessary.

Caldillo (Mexican Stew)

Muriel Bates got this recipe from Paco's mama (see *Spinster's Folly*, Chapter 4), along with the New Mexico chilies. Muriel, as always, passed the recipe—and a stock of chilies—along to her good friend, Julia. It has been modernized for convenience.

~~~

1 tablespoon lard
2 pounds round steak, cubed
1 cup potatoes, diced
1 tablespoon flour
1 medium onion, chopped
1 clove garlic, minced
2 4-ounce cans whole green chilies
1 14-ounce can diced tomatoes
1 teaspoon salt
1/2 teaspoon black pepper
1/2 teaspoon comino (cumin)
2 to 2 1/2 cups hot water

Melt lard in a medium-sized saucepan. Add meat and brown well. Add potatoes and sauté until potatoes are golden brown. Mix in flour well, add onion and garlic. Continue sautéing about 10 minutes, until onions are transparent.

Cut green chilies into large pieces. Add with tomatoes, salt, seasonings, and hot water.

Cover and simmer until potatoes are tender.

~NOTES~

BISCUITS, BREAD, & BREAKFAST BREADS

Baking Powder Biscuits

When she could get wheat to grind for flour, Julia made these biscuits, which delighted her family.

~~~

4 cups sifted flour
3 tablespoons baking powder
2 teaspoons salt
1 1/3 cup milk
2/3 cup melted lard or butter

Sift together dry ingredients; add liquids, mix to a soft dough.

Pat out on floured board to about 1/2-inch thick; cut with round cutter or cut in squares with a knife.

Bake in hot oven (450 F.) until lightly browned. Open, butter, and serve with creamed vegetables or soup. Or, bake on top of a stew. Or, eat with honey or jam.

Corn Meal Biscuits

A more common version of biscuits that Julia made included corn meal.

~~~

1 1/2 cup sifted enriched flour
1/2 cup corn meal
3 teaspoons baking powder
1 teaspoon salt
1/4 cup shortening
2/3 cup milk

Sift together the dry ingredients. Cut in shortening until the mixture resembles coarse crumbs.

Add milk, mixing lightly only until the mixture is dampened. Add a little more milk if necessary, to make a soft dough.

Turn out on lightly floured board and knead gently a few seconds. Roll out to 3/8-inch thickness; cut with floured biscuit cutter.

Bake on an ungreased baking sheet in a very hot oven (450° F.), 12 to 15 minutes. Makes 12 biscuits.

Homestead Loaves

This modernized bread recipe uses packets of yeast, a luxury Julia did not enjoy. Her family enjoyed her warm loaves of bread with supper, though.

~ ~ ~

1 1/2 cups milk
4 tablespoons molasses
3 teaspoons salt
6 tablespoons butter
1 1/2 cups warm water
2 packages dry yeast
7 1/4 cups flour

In a pot, scald the milk. Add molasses, salt and butter. Cool.

In a large bowl add yeast to warm water. Stir in milk mixture.

Add 1/2 of the flour and beat vigorously. Add remaining flour and mix until the dough is soft and pliable.

Place on floured surface and knead until smooth. Shape into a ball. Place in greased bowl and cover. Let rise until twice its size.

Punch down, divide into 2 loaves. Place in greased pans, let rise 1 hour.

Bake 30 minutes in a 375° F. oven. Serves 6 to 8.

Pennsylvania Flannel Cakes

This is one of the "receipts" Julia brought from home when Cousin Camilla asked her to come help prepare for the wedding.

~~~

One quart of milk
Half a teaspoonful of salt.
3 eggs, the whites beaten separately to a stiff froth.

Mix the milk, salt, and yolks, stir in sufficient flour till a batter is made suitable for griddle cakes. Then, when ready to bake, stir in the egg whites.

Rye flour is very fine used in this way instead of wheat, but the cakes adhere so much that it is difficult to bake them. Many love them much better than the wheat.

Sally Lunn - A Sweet Bread

Thinking she'd better become a proper Southerner as soon as possible after her wedding, Julia acquired this recipe from the grocer's wife to try it out on Rod. As the woman gave no directions for baking time or heat, the bread was a sunken failure.

~~~

Seven cups of sifted flour
Half a tea-cup of butter (about 2 ounces), warmed in a pint of milk
One salt teaspoon of salt
3 well-beaten eggs
2 tablespoons brewer's yeast

Pour this into square pans to rise, and then bake it before it sours.

With brewer's or distillery yeast, it will rise in two or three hours, and must not be made over night. With home-brewed yeast, it rises in four or five hours.

~~~

When her friend Muriel came the next day to return a pie plate and found Julia in tears over her sunken loaf of bread, she showed her what she had done wrong:

"After you sift the flour, you must make a hole in the middle and put in the milk and butter, like this. Do you have a salt spoon?"
"No."

"Then use only half a regular spoonful. Put it in your hand and judge the amount before you put it in with the milk and butter. There, that's right. Now, stir it up, so. Have you beaten the eggs?"

Julia passed over the bowl of eggs, and Muriel folded them into the flour mixture.

"There. Where is your yeast?"

"Here." Julia handed her a corked bottle.

Muriel pulled out the cork and sniffed the yeast. "What sort is this?"

"It's milk yeast. I have no other kind."

"Ah! That is why your bread did not rise enough."

"What? How can that be?"

"With milk yeast, you must use twice as much and leave the bread to rise for double the time." Muriel took a small teacup from the shelf and poured in yeast, nearly to the top. "Beat that in while I grease your pan."

"I didn't pay any heed to the yeast," Julia admitted. "I thought milk yeast would serve well." She followed the instructions, beating in the yeast.

When Muriel's task was completed, she turned with the greased pan in her hand and asked, "How hot was your oven?"

Julia looked guiltily at her friend. "I think I did not check."

"Moderate heat is best," Muriel said. "You must build a hot fire in the oven Mr. Owen set into the wall by the fireplace." She gestured toward it, and smiled. "That's very

38

handy. Your man takes care of you."

Julia felt the blood rising into her cheeks and turned away to pour the batter into the pan.

Muriel smiled again and continued. "When the fire burns down, sweep out the ashes and test the heat with your hand. If you can stand the heat for forty-five seconds, put in the bread straight away and shut the door tight. Don't look at it for thirty minutes. Then take a peek to see if it is browned sufficiently. For regular bread, if you thump the loaf and it sounds hollow, it's done."

"I know that."

"Of course you do, Julia. Your Sally Lunn failed for fault of the yeast. This is a good batch. It should have risen by the time Mr. Owen is cleaning up for supper."

Julia cleared her throat. "Thank you for your advice. I do hope this Sally Lunn turns out better than before. I want," she breathed deeply. "I want a sort of celebration."

"Oh?" Muriel waited.

"I have something to tell Mr. Owen."

"Yes?" Muriel's face lit up.

"There is to be a child." Julia knew her cheeks were scarlet from the burning blood she felt in them.

"My dear." Muriel came over and wrapped her arms around Julia. "You are fortunate. My very best wishes."

Julia ducked her head, remembering too late Muriel's childless state. "Thank you. I hope Mr. Owen will be glad."

"He will be over the moon with happiness, Julia. He is so fond of you. I have overheard him talking with Mr. Bates, speaking of wanting sons." She nodded. "He will be pleased."

"I hope I can give him one," Julia whispered, and squeezed Muriel tightly. "I know nothing of infants. I'm so frightened."

Muriel sniffed against the back of her hand. "I am sorry I cannot help you in that matter."

The friends clung together for a moment more, then Muriel gathered her things and departed, leaving Julia in a high state of anticipation for the evening meal.

Miss B.'s Waffles

After Rod's horse-training business took off, he bought Julia a waffle iron so she could bake him these waffles in the fireplace.

~~~

1 quart flour
1 teaspoon salt
1 teaspoon saleratus (baking soda)
1 quart sour milk
2 tablespoons melted butter
5 eggs, well beaten
Some like 1 cup sugar added
Lard

Sift the flour and salt together. Add sugar if you like it.

Mix the melted butter into the milk. Add saleratus to the milk to "sweeten" it.* Gradually mix the milk into the flour, so as not to have lumps. Add the well-beaten eggs.

Bake in waffle irons well-oiled with lard each time they are used. Lay one side on coals, and in about two minutes, turn the other side to the coals.

This actually activates the saleratus in order to raise the waffles.

Fritters - An Old Lee Family Recipe

Julia clipped this recipe, celebrating the victory at Fredericksburg by Gen'l Robert E. Lee, from a Richmond newspaper during the "War Against Northern Aggression".

~~~

Early in the evening, make up 1 quart of flour with 1 egg well beaten, a large spoonful of yeast, and as much milk as will make it a little softer than muffin dough.

In the morning, when well risen, work in 2 tablespoonfuls of melted butter.

Make into balls the size of a walnut and fry a light brown in boiling lard. Serve with wine and sugar or molasses.

CORN BREADS & PUDDING

Virginia Ash Cake

After Rod Owen took his bride home from their surprise wedding, he made this simple recipe and showed Julia how to cook the cakes on the hearth.

~ ~ ~

Add a teaspoonful of salt to a quart of sifted corn meal. Make up with water and knead well. Make into round, flat cakes.

Sweep a clean place on the hottest part of the hearth. Put the cakes on it and cover with hot wood ashes.

Wash and wipe it dry before eating it. Sometimes a cabbage leaf is placed under it, and one over it, before baking, in which case it need not be washed.

Old Fashioned Spoon Bread

This recipe turned out well when Julia chose to make *it* in her quest to become recognized as a citizen of Shenandoah County, Virginia.

~~~

1/2 cup corn meal
2 cups milk
3/4 teaspoon salt
1 tablespoon melted butter
2 egg yolks
2 teaspoons baking powder
2 egg whites

Combine corn meal, milk, salt and butter in saucepan over low heat. Stir constantly until thickened.

Add corn meal mixture to egg yolks slowly, stirring well. Fold in baking powder and beaten egg whites.

Pour into buttered baking dish; bake in a moderate oven (350° F.) about 40 minutes. Serve with butter and gravy.

CHEESE SPOON BREAD

Fold 1 cup (about 1/4 pound) grated cheese into batter when adding beaten egg whites.

HAM OR CHICKEN SPOON BREAD

Fold 1 cup cooked, chopped, chicken or ham into batter with beaten egg whites.

FOR FRYING FISH OR CHICKEN

Dip in mixture of 1 beaten egg and 2 tablespoons milk. Roll in 1 cup corn meal blended with 2 teaspoons salt. Fry.

Corn Muffins

Julia often made breads using corn meal, which was more plentiful than wheat flour in Virginia. But when she could stretch her flour stores, she made these muffins, to which she added fresh berries in summertime. This recipe is one she could make with mulberries or blueberries

~~~

3/4 cup corn meal
3/4 cup sifted flour
2 tablespoons sugar
2 teaspoons baking powder
1/2 teaspoon salt
1 egg
1/2 cup milk
1/3 cup melted butter

Mix dry ingredients in bowl. Beat egg, milk and butter together; add to dry ingredients. Stir only until blended. Fill well-greased muffin tins about two-thirds full of batter. Bake in a hot oven (425° F.) for 20-25 minutes.

FRUIT MUFFINS

Add 1/4 cup fresh berries or peaches to the batter.

Baked Indian Pudding

Corn meal was known as Indian meal while Julia was growing up. It took many years for her to think of it as plain corn meal. She brought this recipe with her from Pennsylvania. Suet is the almost-sweet hard fat from around an animal's loins and kidney area.

~~~

Take nearly one pint sifted [corn] meal to make into a mush. Pour over it one quart of boiled sweet milk. Add 1/2 cup molasses, 1/2 cup sugar, six eggs beaten separately, and half a pint of chopped suet.

If you like, add a few currants, raisins, or a little citron. Bake nearly two hours. Eat topped with lemon sauce.

Lemon Sauce

1 pound sugar
3 ounces butter
1/2 cup water
Juice and sliced rinds of 2 lemons
2 eggs, beaten separately

Pour all but the eggs into a saucepan, and while it is coming to a boil, add the beaten egg yolks. When well boiled, take it from the fire and add the whites of the two eggs, beaten to a froth.

Corn Pone

When Julia saved the corn crop from the Yankees in *The Man from Shenandoah*, her family had little else to eat in the Valley that had been burned bare by Sheridan's army. She may have skimped on the oil and butter in this simple recipe.

~~~

Pour two cups of boiling water into two cups of plain corn meal, stirring constantly until you have a stiff paste (you may season with a little salt and bacon grease if you have it). Shape into small pones or ovals and fry in hot oil until nice and brown. Serve hot with plenty of butter.

Green Corn Patties
(Mock Oysters)

James brought this recipe home from war. He had been introduced to oysters when he fought in eastern Virginia, but during the siege of Petersburg, he and his comrades had to make do with green corn cakes instead.

~~~

1 egg, beaten
2 tablespoons flour
12 ears of sweet white corn, grated (yellow corn will do, but not so well.)
1 teaspoon salt
1 teaspoon pepper
Butter or sweet lard

Beat the egg into the flour. Mix all ingredients; make into small cakes and fry until brown in butter or lard.

~NOTES~

JELLIES & DRIED FRUITS

Apple Jelly

Julia adapted her apple jelly recipe to make jellies of other local fruit, like grapes and Damson plums.

~~~

Take the best pippins and wipe them, taking out stem and eye. Cut them in thin slices, without paring or quartering, as the chief flavor is in the peel, and the jelly part is in the cores.

Put them in a preserving kettle and put in just water enough to cover them. Boil them very soft, then mash and strain through a jelly-bag made of coarse flannel.

Put the liquid into the kettle with a pint of brown sugar to each pint of the liquid, and add the juice and rind of a lemon cut in slices.

Beat up the white of one egg and stir in very thoroughly.

Boil up 3 times, throwing in some cold water to stop it from running over. Let it stand quiet on the hearth half an hour. Try it, and if not hard enough, let it boil till it will turn to jelly on cooling.

Skim off the scum and pour off the clear jelly. Strain the sediment through the jelly-bag. Then put it in glasses.

It can be boiled down and make elegant apple candy.

Grapes and Damson plums should have water put in when first boiled, as the flavor is thus more perfectly extracted. Frost grapes make an elegant jelly, as do the wild plum, by this method. In summer, these jellies are fine for effervescing drinks, with some good wine vinegar mixed with them.

~NOTES~

Calf's Foot Jelly

Julia was quite surprised when Rod brought a set of calf's feet into the kitchen after he traded the training of a horse for a butchered beef, and asked her to make jelly of them. She figured out a way to do it.

~ ~ ~

To four nicely-cleaned calf's feet, put four quarts of water; let it simmer gently till reduced to two quarts, then strain it, and let it stand all night.

Take off all the fat and sediment, melt it, add the juice of three lemons, then the peels, a pint of wine, the whites of four eggs, three sticks of cinnamon, and sugar to taste.

Boil ten minutes, then skim out the spice and lemon peel, and strain it.

An alternative is to use gelatin, which only needs to be dissolved in hot water, sweetened, and flavored.

Cooking Dried Fruits

To give variety to her winter meals, Julia would stew dried fruits that she had preserved the previous fall.

~~~

The following mode of cooking dried fruits is the best. Take dried peaches, quinces, or apples, and put them to swell in cold water for several hours. Peaches must be very thoroughly washed. Then put them into a stewing kettle with a great deal of water, and a pint of brown sugar to each pound of fruit. Cover them, and let them simmer very slowly for several hours, till the water is boiled down to as much liquid as you wish.

Peaches have a finer flavor when dried with the skin on, as fully ripe peaches cannot be pared and dried. When finely flavored, peaches have a solid pulp; when ripe, they should be pared and then dried, and such are much the best for cooking in the above way.

They will, when cooked thus, be preferred by everybody to the finest and most expensive sweetmeats.

DESSERTS

Ginger Snaps

Rod felt convinced he had made the right choice in asking Julia to marry him when he tasted her ginger cookies. This modernized recipe makes about 5 dozen.

~~~

2 1/3 cups flour
1/2 teaspoon salt
2 teaspoons baking soda
1 teaspoon ground cinnamon
1/2 teaspoon ground mace
1 to 2 teaspoons ground ginger, as desired
3/4 cups lard
1 cup sugar
1 egg
1/3 cup molasses
granulated sugar for coating

Sift together the flour, salt, baking soda, and spices and set aside.

Cream the lard and sugar until light, beat in egg. Add molasses, beating well. Add the sifted dry ingredients.

Form into small 1-inch balls and roll in granulated sugar. Place cookies about 1 1/2 inches apart on ungreased baking sheets. Bake in a moderate 350° F. oven until light brown and fluffy, about 10 minutes. Remove at once to wire racks to cool or cool on baking sheets.

Lard Pastry

The education of every 19th century girl included learning to make pastry. Aunt Susannah taught Julia this art on one of her summer visits. Makes two single pie crusts, one double pie crust, or 6 to 8 tart shells.

~~~

2 cups flour
1 teaspoon salt
2/3 cup lard
5 to 7 tablespoons ice water

Sift flour and salt together in bowl.

Cut in lard with pastry blender, two knives, or a blending fork, until pieces are the size of small peas. Add cold water a few drops at a time until particles just hold together. Press together lightly to form a ball. Chill for easier handling.

Divide pastry in half. Roll 1/8-inch thick and line a pie pan. For a single crust pastry, trim 1/2 inch beyond the edge. Fold under and flute edge of pastry. Prick pastry with a fork before baking. Bake at 450° F. for 8 to 10 minutes.

For a double crust pie, roll the other half of the pastry, making several slits in the top crust. Place over filling and cut 1/2 inch smaller than lower crust. Fold lower crust over top crust and flute edges. Bake according to pie recipe.

Apple Pie

When Julia decided to make an apple pie to enter in the Shenandoah County Fair, this is the recipe she used.

~ ~ ~

Pare and slice apples.

Make a little thick syrup of white sugar, into which throw a few cloves, allspice, or mace, as you prefer. In this syrup, scald a few apples at a time, taking them out and putting more in till all are slightly cooked.

Set aside to cool, then pour into deep pie plates lined with pastry. Sprinkle with flour. Put bits of butter over all. Sprinkle with flour again. Cover with pastry and bake.

Soda Cracker (Mock Apple) Pie

Toward the end of the war, when apple trees had been cut down for firewood (see *Gone for a Soldier*), Julia learned to make this recipe. The soda crackers of the war era were large, hard crackers much like soldier's hard tack. James reported that in order not to crack his teeth, he had to crush his tack on a rock with his rifle butt to get small pieces he could soak in water long enough to soften it all up to eat. Recipe makes a 9-inch pie.

~~~

Pour water on two large or four round soda crackers (or a dozen saltine crackers) and let them remain till thoroughly wet. Press out the water and crush them up together.

Stir in the juice and the grated peel of a lemon, with a cup or more of powdered sugar. Put in pastry and bake at 350° F. for 30 minutes.

Berry Pie

When Marie and Julianna Owen and Ellen Bates went to pick blackberries in *The Man from Shenandoah*, this was the dessert they intended to make.

~~~

4-6 tablespoons flour
1 cup sugar
Dash cinnamon or nutmeg
3 cups berries
1 tablespoon butter
1 tablespoon lemon juice
Unbaked double pie crust

Blend sifted dry ingredients together and mix with fruit.

Pile into unbaked crust, dot with butter, sprinkle with lemon juice and top with pricked crust or strips of pastry in crisscross fashion. Bake 30-45 minutes at 425° F.

This recipe may be used for huckleberry, raspberry, blackberry, peach, green apple, and cherry pies.

Texas Pudding

Bill Henry taught this recipe to Marie. She shared it with Julia later.

~~~

3 eggs (yolks and whites beaten separately)
3 cups sugar
1 cup butter
1 cup sweet milk
2 tablespoons flour

Bake in a crust. This will fill three pie-plates.

MISCELLANEOUS RECIPES & FRONTIER WISDOM

Odd Ingredients

Julia grew up knowing her lard from her suet, but those terms for fat are almost unknown in our day. Few people know what saleratus is. You will, shortly.

~~~

What is lard? Lard is pig fat.

What is suet? Suet is the raw, hard fat of beef or mutton found around the loins and kidneys of cattle or sheep.

What is saleratus? Saleratus was an early form of baking soda.

Wine Substitutions

Wine was quite often used in vintage recipes, and Julia occasionally made frugal use of it.

Instead of red wine, you may use grape, pomegranate, or cranberry juice, or chicken, beef, or vegetable stock. Add a tablespoon of vinegar or lemon juice per cup of juice for a punchier substitute, and for more flavor, add a tablespoon of vinegar per cup of stock.

Instead of white wine, you could try lemon juice, white grape juice, or chicken or vegetable stock. Dilute the lemon juice with the same amount of water to prevent an overpowering experience.

Again, punch up the impact of grape juice by adding a tablespoon of vinegar or lemon juice per cup of juice. Make the stocks more flavorful with a tablespoon of lemon juice or vinegar mixed in.

Home-Brewed Yeast

In the days before foil packets of dry yeast, Julia had to manufacture her own for raising bread.

~~~

POTATO YEAST

By those who use potato yeast, it is regarded as much the best, as it raises bread quicker than common home-brewed yeast, and best of all, never imparts the sharp, disagreeable yeast taste to bread or cake, often given by hop yeast.

Mash half a dozen peeled boiled potatoes, and mix in a handful of wheat flour and two teaspoons of salt. After putting it through a colander, add hot water till it is a batter. When blood warm, put in half a tea-cup of distillery yeast, or twice as much potato, or other home-brewed.

When raised, keep it corked tight, and make it new very often in hot weather.

MILK YEAST
(when no other yeast is to be had)

1 pint of new milk
1 teaspoon of fine salt
1 large spoonful (tablespoon) of flour.

Mix, and keep it blood warm an hour. Use twice as much as the common yeast. Bread made of this soon spoils.

MARSHA WARD

Keeping Meat Fresh

Keeping meat from spoiling was an everyday
worry, but especially on the frontier of
Colorado Territory in the summertime. Julia
had to employ this method of keeping game
fresh.

~~~

In summertime, meat will not stay fresh
for many hours. However, it may be
preserved overnight by sprinkling it with a
little salt and placing it in a wet, tightly
woven bag of thin cloth. See that flies
cannot go through the cloth. Hang the bag
in a current of air, out of reach of animals.

Cottage Cheese

Here are two methods of making cottage cheese that Julia used, depending on whether she had buttermilk or not.

~~~

When the tea-kettle boils, pour the water into a pan of "loppered"* milk. It will curdle at once. Stir it and turn it into a colander, pour a little cold water over it, salt it and break it up.

A better way is to put equal parts of buttermilk and thick milk into a kettle, and over the fire, heat it almost boiling hot. Pour into a linen bag and let it drain till next day. Then take it out, salt it, put in a little cream or butter, as it may be thick or not, and make it up into little balls the size of an orange.

*Loppered milk is the thick, soured milk left behind in a milk pan, dish, or pail after the cream has been skimmed from the top. Milk typically was set out for one to three days, depending on the season, so the cream would rise out of it.

Preserving Butter

Butter can go bad in the summertime. Julia got Rod and the boys to dig a pit and bury a barrel in the earth for a temporary "refrigerator" when they first arrived in Colorado Territory.

~~~

After making butter, enclose it in a tight tin or a wooden box. In hot weather, butter will keep for several weeks sunk in a strong brine, or kept in a cool place, such as a spring house, a root cellar, or for want of a cellar, in a barrel sunk into the earth in a shaded, dry location.

Homemade Lye & Concentrated Lye Soap

All women of the era who desired to wash clothing or their persons learned to make soap with lye, usually of their own manufacture. Julia was no exception. Her daughter-in-law Mary made soap in the garden, as she recounted to Rulon in a letter in *Gone for a Soldier*.

~~~

Lye

Do not use aluminum pots or pans; the lye will eat through them.

Boil ashes from a hardwood fire in soft water, such as rain water, for half an hour. Allow the ashes to settle to the bottom of the pan. Skim the liquid lye from the top; collect in an appropriate vessel.

Repeat daily until you have enough of the weak solution to boil down until it will float an egg or small potato.

Concentrated Lye Soap

All fat and grease from the kitchen should be carefully saved, and should be made into soap before accumulating and becoming offensive.

Boil for six hours 10 gallons of lye made of green wood ashes. Then add 8 or 10 pounds of grease, and continue to boil it. If thick and ropy, add more lye till the grease is absorbed. This is ascertained by dropping a spoonful in a glass of water, and if the grease remains it will show on the water.

If hard soap is desired, put 1 quart of salt in a half-gallon of hot water. Stir till dissolved and pour into the boiling soap. Boil 20 minutes, stirring continually.

Remove from the fire, pour into molds or a wooden box,* and when cold, cut in cakes and dry.

A box of concentrated lye may be used instead of salt, as it will obviate the necessity of using more dripped lye to consume the grease.

Soft soap is made the same way, but without the addition of salt or concentrated lye to the mixture.

*Use a wooden box mold for a bar of soap, two inches high, three inches wide, and six inches long. Or use a larger box, and cover the bottom of the mold with waxed paper or grease to prevent sticking.

RECIPE SOURCES

Beecher, Catharine E., *Miss Beecher's Domestic Receipt-Book* (Third Edition). Harper & Brothers, Publishers, New York, 1858. Reprint. Dover Publications, Inc. Mineola, New York, 2001.

Bomberger, Maude A., *Colonial Recipes: From Old Virginia and Maryland Manors*. The Neale Publishing Company, New York and Washington, 1907.

Gould, John Mead, *How to Camp Out*. 1877.

Williams, Nyla Allphin and Emily Williams, Compilers and Editors, *The Orin G. Williams Centennial Cookbook*. October 4, 2000.

The Virginia Federation of Home Demonstration Clubs, Compilers, *Recipes from Old Virginia*. The Dietz Press, Incorporated, Richmond, Virginia, 1958.

Tyree, Marion Cabell, Ed., *Housekeeping in Old Virginia*. John P. Morton and Company, Louisville, KY, 1879. Reprint. Favorite Recipes Press, Inc., Louisville, KY, 1965.

Ward, Marsha, Personal Recipe Collection.

Thank You!

Please post a review of this book on your favorite review or purchase site. Reviews from readers, even as few as twenty words, make all the difference to those browsing and buying.

Remember to recommend this book to your friends, telling them what you liked about it. Word-of-mouth recommendations are valuable rewards for authors.

Finally, subscribe to Marsha's VMA Readers email list to receive advance notice of coming book releases.
https://is.gd/rBXkA4

About the Author

Marsha Ward writes authentic historical fiction set in 19th Century America, and contemporary romance. She was born in the sleepy little town of Phoenix, Arizona, in a simpler time. With plenty of room to roam among the chickens and citrus trees, Marsha enjoyed playing with neighborhood chums, but always had her imaginary friend, cowboy Johnny Rigger Prescott, at her side. Now she makes her home in a forest in the mountains of Arizona. She loves to hear from her readers.

Connect with her at:

Website: http://marshaward.com
Blog: http://marshaward.blogspot.com
Email: marshaw@marshaward.com
Facebook:
https://www.facebook.com/authormarshaward
Twitter: https://twitter.com/MarshaWard

Do subscribe to Marsha's VMA Readers email list to receive advance notice of coming book releases. https://is.gd/rBXkA4